Secrets
of
Life

Secrets of Life

of

J. Donald Walters

WARNER BOOKS

A Time Warner Company

Warner Books, Inc., 1271 Avenue of the Americas, New York, NY 10020

W A Time Warner Company

Printed in the United States of America
First Printing: September 1994
10   9   8   7   6   5   4   3   2   1

Library of Congress Cataloging-in-Publication Data

Walters, J. Donald.
    Secrets of life / J. Donald Walters.
        p.   cm.
    ISBN 0-446-51864-6
    1. Life.   2. Conduct of life.   I. Title.
BD431.W2264   1994
170'.44—dc20   94-3813
                                        CIP

*Life is
the quest
for joy.*

—J. DONALD WALTERS

Contents

Secrets
of
Life

Introduction

There are two ways of looking at people: outwardly, and from within.

The outer view is bewilderingly complex—a study of contrasts and differences, of countless relationships and relativities. It is the "thumbprint" view. For just as every thumbprint is unique, so every human being differs in innumerable ways from every other. Specific genetic pattern, upbringing, environment, personality, interests, and myriads of other factors stamp each one as one of a kind. Looking at people from without, it seems almost unbelievable that they can even communicate together!

My own case may be an exaggerated example. My parents were born in Oklahoma, but my father, an oil geologist, was stationed in Romania, where I was born. I grew up there, cut off in many ways from what we in America think of as the Twentieth Century. At nine I was sent away to school in Switzerland; later, in England. We were in America on vacation when World War II broke out, so we remained here. Much more recently, in 1976, I wrote an autobiography called *The Path*.[1] Before writing it, I wondered whether my life wouldn't be considered so different from other people's that no one would be able to relate to it. Because I wanted my book to communicate with others, and not to be a merely personal declaration, I pondered every instance in my life as something that had happened not uniquely to me, but to me as an example of humanity. I tried to show how my experiences had affected me in ways that I

---

[1]Crystal Clarity, Publisher, Nevada City, CA. Distributed by Warner Books.

could share with everyone. It has been gratifying to me, over the years, to receive many hundreds of letters from people who wrote to say in effect, "Your book was the story of *my* life."

*F*or there is that second view of human life and of human nature: the inner view.

*I*n a sense, each of us (John Donne notwithstanding) *is* an island. In another sense, however, we are all one. For though islands appear separate, and may even be situated at great distances from one another, they are only extrusions of the same planet, Earth.

A resident of, let us say, Tulsa, Oklahoma, may want his meat and potatoes. A native Hawaiian may prefer poi. A resident of India may insist on eating curry. All of them, however, require their daily sustenance.

*T*here are realities we all share, regardless of our nationality, language, or individual tastes. As we need food, so do we need emotional nourishment: love, kindness, appreciation, and support from others. We need to understand our environment and our relationship to it. We need to fulfill certain inner hungers: the need for happiness, for peace of mind—for wisdom.

A reality we all share is our egos. Reality, as far as each of us is concerned, is centered in ourselves. Science may never be able to locate the center of the universe, but as far as each of us is concerned, *we*, individually, *are* the center of the universe!

*Y*et we know that there is a vast reality out there to be explored, and if possible to be understood. Some of us reach out toward it, to embrace it. We want to know how this little ego of ours relates to the vastness around us. We want to know how our realities fit in with those of other people—how our ego relates to other egos. Maturity in a human being is the ability to relate to other realities than one's own. The more encompassing a person's vision, the deeper his maturity and wisdom.

Others of us, however, seek protection from what they perceive as a threat in all that vastness: not only the universe, but the vast diversity of human customs, attitudes, desires, and ideas; in short, other people's realities.

If our effort is to reach outward from our egos to a broader reality, our consciousness and self-identity expand. If, on the contrary, we try to enclose ourselves protectively against our environment or against other people, our consciousness and self-identity contract.

The simple fact is that, the more expansive our consciousness, the happier we feel, and the more self-fulfilled. But the more contractive our outlook, the more unhappy, frustrated, even bitter we become. The explanation lies in the fact that, although born with egos, all of us are part of, and *belong to*, a universal reality. We are self-fulfilled to the degree that we partake of that reality. And we offend against our own deepest nature when we divorce ourselves from that reality.

On these simple thoughts was this book written. Truth *is* simple. It is the ego that likes to complicate it, so as to feed its pride in its own intelligence. My own experience in life is that, until a person can simplify an idea to the point where others, when they hear it, cry, "Of course!" he hasn't fully understood it yet, himself.

I suggest you take one thought at a time from the following pages. Keep it before you throughout the day, as a reminder. Repeat it out loud, or mentally, letting it sink into your subconscious. And look for situations in your life to which you can apply it creatively.

*F*or what I've tried to do in offering these seed thoughts is make *you* coauthor of this book. I've done my best not to do your thinking for you. But I've tried to put these thoughts in such a way as to inspire you to think, "So *that's* what that experience (or those experiences) in my life meant!"

Happiness

*H*appiness is the innocent enjoyment of simple things.

*H*appiness is seeing your work as service.

*H*appiness is a smile of comfort to the sorrowful.

*H*appiness is a heart kept open to the stranger.

*H*appiness is working with other people's realities, with their natures as they are, and not trying to force them into a mold of your own making.

*H*appiness is including other people's happiness in your own.

*H*appiness is understanding that friendship is more precious than mere things, more precious than getting your own way, more precious than being right in situations where true principles are not at stake.

*H*appiness is accepting whatever comes, with an attitude of calm, inner freedom.

Happiness is finding love through giving love, rather than through receiving it.

*H*appiness is a pure heart, empty of malice and self-seeking.

*H*appiness is the determination to *be* happy always, rather than wait for outer circumstances to make you happy.

*H*appiness is even-mindedness through all the storms of life.

*H*appiness is living in, but not for, the moment—in the Eternal Now.

*H*appiness is giving up personal attachments, recognizing that nothing and no one truly belongs to us, since all is God's.

*H*appiness is reverence for all life.

*H*appiness is loyalty to your own, then gradually expanding that loyalty to include all beings as your own.

*H*appiness is a humble heart, free from pretensions, aware that nothing man can do is of everlasting importance.

*H*appiness is worshiping God everywhere, in everything.

*H*appiness is laughing with others, not at them.

*H*appiness is kindness, seeing others as extensions of your own self.

*H*appiness is doing joyfully and willingly whatever needs to be done.

*H*appiness is the desire to learn, rather than to teach.

Happiness is the ability to congratulate yourself happily on your own unimportance while others vie together for supremacy.

Happiness is understanding that man's highest duty is to love.

Happiness is smiling with the heart and the eyes, not merely with the lips.

Happiness is seeking to help others rather than to be helped by them.

Happiness is strengthening others' faith in themselves, and in their own high potential.

*H*appiness is being grateful for the hurts you receive, for they are channels of understanding and wisdom.

*H*appiness is relinquishing the sense of "I" and "mine."

*H*appiness is a heart reaching out to embrace all mankind as brothers and sisters.

*H*appiness is love.

Love

*L*ove is a blend of informality and courtesy. Courtesy is not diplomacy; it is a mark of thoughtfulness and sensitivity. Between two persons who love each other, courtesy, like a delicate waterfall, keeps the mountain pool of their love ever fresh.

*S*how respect for one another. For while feelings fluctuate, respect can remain a constant. Listen respectfully to your partner's views when they differ from your own. Preserve a certain dignity in your relationship: that dignity which gives others freedom to be themselves.

*D*on't make demands of each other. Love that is not freely given is bondage.

Love

*P*erform some little act daily to give happiness to your beloved: an act of service, perhaps; a small gift; a word of appreciation; a special smile of affection. Let not the happy brook of your love run dry for lack of replenishing rain.

*B*e creative in your relationship. Tend it lovingly, like a garden. Keep it seeded with fresh interests, fresh ideas. Help it to grow always more beautiful. Weed it regularly, lest the flower beds become overrun with the rank growth of unconscious habits. For love to be ever new, it must be approached creatively, as an art.

*K*eep a sense of humor. Share together a sense of the absurd. At the same time, be careful how you tease each other. Never tease if the teasing is unappreciated. Let your humor be kindly, never sarcastic.

*N*ever lose sight of the underlying reality of your love. Reflect: Isn't your long-term relationship more important than any passing disagreement? Flow with the longer rhythms of your love.

*D*evelop charitable attitudes. Anger is an inner recognition of impotence, but charity is an inner recognition of strength.

Love

*A*void voicing negative emotions. Wait, rather, for calmness to return. When you are upset, you perceive few things with clarity, though Emotion parade itself in the garb of revelation. Calm your heart's feelings· Only in calmness can you perceive things as they really are.

*S*how appreciation when you feel it. Never take your beloved's awareness of this sentiment for granted. Though the sentiment is as old as the human race, no matter how often you say with sincere feeling, "I love you," your words will sound forever fresh, forever new.

*H*old hands together in silence. You will learn gradually to communicate with one another telepathically.

Develop reverence—less for each other than for Love itself, the eternal gift of God.

*P*ay more attention to the tones of your voice. To magnetize the voice, lift it up from the heart, then release it to soar outward through the forehead. Keep the vocal cords relaxed. Your voice will be a delight to listen to, if

you express through it the calm
feelings of your heart.

*S*peak more with the eyes—"the
windows of the soul." If you use
your eyes when speaking, it will
be as if those windows were
framed with colorful curtains,
making the home warm
and inviting.

*H*old realistic expectations
of one another. After all,
imperfection is inherent in
humanity. Concentrate on the
qualities that drew you both
together, not on others that might
force you apart.

*D*on't be possessive. Reflect that
no one ever truly owns another

Love

human being. Don't bind your
beloved with the cord of your
own needs. A plant flourishes
when it is given free access to air
and sunlight.

*T*ry not to reshape your partner
into a mold of your own making.
Criticism is corrosive. Accept
what *is*, and both of you will be
happier. A good rule is this:
Encourage the strengths you see,
but neither feed nor cauterize
the weaknesses.

*W*hen misunderstandings occur,
don't dwell on how your partner
has disappointed you. Ask
yourself, rather, "What can I
do to change *myself*—so such

misunderstandings will not
occur again?"

Love

*N*either of you should assume
the role of teacher to the other,
where personal issues are
concerned. On the other hand, be
grateful for anything you can
learn from your beloved.

*W*henever you feel inspired to
make a suggestion, concentrate
not on your own need to make it,
but on the other person's need to
hear it. Wait even then—for
months, if need be—until you
perceive in your partner a
readiness to hear what you
have to say.

*S*hare with one another your deeper beliefs, your ideals, your aspirations.

*E*njoy stillness together, for in stillness love attains perfection. Love is not passion. Human love is a reflection of divine love. And God is perfect stillness.

*L*ove God in each other. Thus, you will feel always drawn to the divine perfection behind the human error. For humanity struggles, in the face of countless obstacles and by many and various routes, toward ideals that are universal and eternal.

*E*xpand your love for each other until it transcends human love—until it embraces all humanity, all living creatures, all things, as the Creator's handiwork.

Love

*G*ive pleasure to each other, but don't demand it in return. For true love is not desire. The stronger the passion, the greater its demands; and the stronger passion's demands, the greater its emphasis on self-love. Not in passion, but in tenderness, in kindness, love finds its ideal expression.

*P*ractice consideration. To whatever extent you show consideration to others, show twice as much to your beloved.

Concentrate on the magnetism you share together. This magnetism is the subtle power that each of you feels from the other. Only in mutual sharing can the magnetism grow.

Seek variety in your life together. Never let routine chords dull the melody of your romance.

Seek opportunities to relax together, to share your interests and ideas. Don't depend too much on outer stimuli for entertainment. (The louder the noise, the hollower the drum!) Be alone together when you can, simply to be yourselves.

_D_evelop adaptability. Keep your love fluid, that it fill whatever vessel life places before you.

Love

_G_ive strength and comfort to your beloved. Receive strength and comfort gratefully in return, while never demanding them.

_B_e steadfast. Keep your love immovable, like a high mountain. Keep it, like rich soil, ever fertile through the changing seasons of your lives. And keep it ever central, like the sun, around which the planets move through endless reaches of time and space.

Friendship

*E*xercise discrimination in your choice of friends. Prefer sincerity over praise, and loyalty over gay smiles.

*R*ealize that to have friends one must first *be* a friend. Make friendship a priority in your life.

*D*emand nothing of others, but act and react together in a spirit of freedom.

*I*nclude other people's happiness in your own.

*B*e more interested in listening to others than in getting them to hear what you have to say.

Friendship

*B*e actively concerned for the well-being of others. Don't limit your concern to mere verbal expressions.

Like others. Don't worry too much over how well they like you.

Show your appreciation. Don't take it for granted that your friends always know how you feel about them.

Accept your friends as they are. Don't try to re-create them in your own image or according to your own desires.

Don't impose your moods, whether good or bad, on others. Give them the space to define their own feelings.

Subordinate your needs to the needs of others. Find in friendship itself your own fulfillment.

Never belittle a friend's enthusiasms.

Be courteous, even to your closest friends. Respect other people's right to their own point of view.

Friendship

Accept good-naturedly, with appreciation, whatever differences exist between you.

Express kindness with your eyes, and through the tone of your voice, not only with your choice of words.

Share with your friends your aspirations and ideals. Do not pass time with them only in merry camaraderie.

When conversing with your friends, give them your full attention.

Hold kind thoughts toward others, especially at those times when misunderstandings occur.

Never judge others. When tempted to do so, concentrate on what attracts you in your friends.

Don't criticize, but sincerely voice the beneficial truth.

Rejoice in your friends' good fortune. Never draw unfavorable

comparisons between their
condition and your own.

Give your friends strength and
understanding in their sorrows,
but don't share their grief so
deeply that you intensify it.

Support your friends in the truth,
no less so if it means confessing
your own error.

An important key to friendship
is reliability. Be true to your
word, to your promises, to
your commitments.

Look always for ways to learn and grow in your association with others.

Seek transcendence in your relationships. See in friendship a window to infinity.

Love God above all. See God's love behind the blessings that are your friends.

By yourself, always. Don't be a mere mirror to your friends.

Don't emphasize the present tensions in your relationships,

when they occur. Concentrate
rather on friendship's
longer rhythms.

Friendship

*F*riendship should be founded on
a bedrock of loyalty. Be a true
friend to others, even when they
let you down.

*S*eek benefits that are mutual.
Never use a friend for your own
selfish ends.

Inner Peace

*P*eace is a quiet heart, its feelings not dependent on outer circumstances.

*P*eace comes with self-control. Don't scatter your energies, but hold their reins in your hands, and manage them usefully.

*P*eace comes from giving your full, interested attention to everything you do.

*P*eace comes through living fully in the moment, releasing past and future into cycles of eternity.

*P*eace comes when you are
inwardly relaxed—physically first,
then emotionally, mentally, and,
finally, spiritually.

Inner
Peace

*P*eace comes with nonattachment.
Remind yourself always that
nothing and no one truly belongs
to you.

*P*eace comes with contentment.
Make it a point consciously to
hold happy thoughts.

*G*ive up unnecessary desires.
Realize that happiness is within

you, not in outward things
or circumstances.

*A*ccept things as they are. Then,
if necessary, act calmly and
cheerfully to improve them.

*Realize that you cannot change the world.
But you* can *change yourself.*

*C*ultivate harmonious friendships.
Shun the company of
peaceless persons.

*P*roject peace outward from your
heart into your environment.

*L*ive simply. Reduce your
definition of life's "necessities."

*L*ive healthfully. Exercise
regularly, eat properly,
breathe deeply.

*P*eace comes with a clear
conscience. Be ever true to
your ideals.

*A*ct from your inner center, in
freedom. Don't live in bondage to
the demands the world makes
of you.

*M*ake truth, in every
circumstance, your guide.

*N*ever covet what others have.
Know that what is yours by right
will most surely find its way to
you if you do your part willingly,
without anxiety, to attract it.

*N*ever complain. Acknowledge
that whatever life gives you
depends on what you give, first,
of yourself.

*A*ccept responsibility for your
failures. Take courage from the
fact that only you can turn them
to success.

*P*eace is found through self-
conquest. It doesn't come with
the mere cessation of hostilities.

*P*eace comes with an attitude of willingness, especially when your mental habits urge you to cry "No!"

Inner Peace

*S*mile in your heart, even if others around you are scowling.

*G*ive joy. But don't demand joy of others.

*P*eace comes from including others' well-being in your own.

*W*ish injury to no one. Never deliberately hurt another human being.

*W*ork *with* others, never against them.

*M*editate daily, to tap the wellsprings of soul-peace.

*R*aise your consciousness. Direct energy upward to the brain. Then center that energy in the seat of higher awareness, in the forehead between the eyebrows.

Peace comes with self-acceptance. Be not blind to your own faults, and don't hate yourself for them, but claim your higher reality in the Infinite Light.

*L*ove God. Strive, in peace, to be worthy of His love.

*P*eace comes when we love others for *their* good, not for our own. There is no peace in harboring selfish motives.

Inner Peace

Prosperity

*T*rue prosperity is contentment.
It is not a bank account.

*P*rosperity is inner happiness.
Outer prosperity follows from a
determination to *be* happy,
always.

*P*rosperity is the fruit of
generosity. Share with others
whatever good life gives you, and
you will open up the wellsprings
of infinite abundance.

*I*nclude the good of others in
your own quest for abundance.

Recognize that you are an instrument in the great Orchestra of Life. All Life will sustain you, if you attune yourself to its harmonies.

Prosperity

Work with, not against, life's changing rhythms. Sometimes, failure itself is only a doorway to new definitions of prosperity.

Look behind the obstacles you face in life. They may prove to be windows of opportunity.

See failures as correctives, merely, not as misfortunes. Be an artist of life, striving ever to perfect your masterpiece.

Diversify not only your financial investments, as monetary counselors advise, but more importantly your investments of energy. Cultivate ever-fresh ideas, fresh interests, fresh relationships—fresh reasons, above all, for enjoying life.

Prosperity requires that you develop faith—faith in yourself; faith in others; faith in life's abundance.

To achieve prosperity, break the hypnosis of self-limitation. The heights that any man has attained can be attained again by others.

They can be attained by anyone, though each in his own way. They can be attained by *you*, given sufficient time, dedication, and directed energy.

Prosperity

*P*rosperity won't come with wishful thinking. Don't fritter energy away on trivial desires. Drop by drop, a leaky faucet wastes many gallons.

*T*rue prosperity is finding pleasure in simplicity.

*H*old positive expectations of life. Support them by a dynamic will.

*S*ee people as your best
investment. Be a true friend to all.

*R*ealize that what you own is
merely held by you in trust. Treat
it responsibly. For if you squander
it, the trust will pass to another.

*P*rosperity is a state of mind,
primarily. Find strength in
yourself. Wait not for the passing
waves of circumstance to propel
you forward.

*R*ealize that you cannot truly
prosper through the diminishment
of others. Help everyone.

Prosperity is a continuous
expansion of your self-identity.

Prosperity

*P*rosperity must be seen as a
universal good. Extend a willing
hand to the needy. Help them
above all to help themselves.

*N*ever help others without giving
them an opportunity to
reciprocate in some way.

*T*he road to prosperity is paved
with common sense. Depend not
on luck, but on a realistic
assessment of the situations you
face. By practical stages, you can

transform "improbables"
into realities.

*R*emember: The higher the
mountain, the harder the effort
required to conquer it. Success is
not for the weakhearted: It is for
those who will never rest until
they attain their ideals.

*B*e willing to sacrifice
nonessentials in your quest
for perfection.

*L*ive in the present, not in
past attainments, nor in
future victories.

*H*ave the patience to adjust action to reality. In every setback, try to understand what lessons you have to learn—from life, from circumstances.

*E*nvy no one. View other people's successes and failures empathetically, as if they were your own.

*P*rosperity is not things; it is a state of mind. Some people are more prosperous owning nothing than others with millions of dollars.

*O*ne secret for achieving prosperity is inventiveness.

Success in any field demands that you develop the creative outlook of an artist. The achievement of true prosperity, indeed, *is* an art.

*F*eed your prosperity daily with fresh thoughts and new ideas— lest, like a still pond, it stagnate.

*U*se your prosperity for the good of all. Never enclose it with self-satisfaction, lest *you* stagnate.

*K*eep a sense of proportion. Obsessions are a narrowing pathway to failure.

*M*ake time in every day for
singing, and for song. Prosperity
that excludes song and laughter
soon turns to obsession.

Prosperity

*R*emember, the less importance
you claim for yourself, the more
importance you will acquire in the
eyes of others. The friendship of
others will in time show itself to
be your greatest asset.

Success

Enjoy, don't regret, the effort required to achieve success.

Do things not merely because they are popular, but because you deeply believe in them.

Work with things as they *are*, not with the way you wish they were, or think they ought to be.

Don't be attached to the results of what you do. Do your best at every moment. The results will then take care of themselves.

Be enthusiastic! Without enthusiasm, nothing worthwhile was ever accomplished.

*A*sk yourself always, not, "What do I want to make happen?" but, "What is it that is trying to happen here?"

*S*ee your work primarily as a service to others, not as a means to personal profit.

*B*lame no one if anything goes wrong. Do what you can, simply, to improve matters.

*B*e crystal clear in your own mind as to your aims and directions. What, specifically, do you want? Why do you want it? What further ends would it serve? Is it

57

a worthwhile goal? Will it hurt
anyone? (If so, abandon it.)
Will it advance your
long-range purposes?

*H*ave the courage of your
convictions. Don't listen to
doubts, if they paralyze you to
inaction. On the other hand, be
open to the truth, from whatever
source it comes.

*Welcome as opportunities the obstacles
that confront you.*

*L*ook upon setbacks as but
stepping-stones to success.

*D*evelop willpower. Set yourself increasingly difficult goals, then persevere until each of them has been achieved.

*B*e energy-oriented rather than goal-oriented. See life in terms of constant progress in an intended direction, not in terms of preestablished ends.

*D*are to step outside the boundaries of conventional wisdom.

*C*oncentrate single-mindedly on whatever task you set yourself.

*V*iew each day as a fresh beginning in your life, bright with promise and expectancy. Never define yourself in terms of your past accomplishments.

*D*o not limit your self-identity to present realities. Expand it constantly, to unfold your highest potentials.

*B*e always ready to reexamine your first principles.

*S*ee that the outcome of everything you do is harmonious. Act always, therefore, with a harmonious, positive attitude.

*A*sk yourself, in the things you do, not merely, "What would people like from me?" but, "What would I feel happy giving them?"

*K*eep your mind open to the truth, however unwelcome or unpalatable.

*P*refer the truth over opinions—even if the opinions be your own.

*C*onsult your inner heart's feelings before you make a decision. Never do a thing, whatever Reason tells you, unless your heart concurs. For the heart

is the seat of intuition, and
intuition transcends reason as the
sun outshines all the stars.

*N*ever make important decisions
when influenced by emotion.
Keep your heart's feelings in a
state of calm reason.

*B*e solution-oriented, not
problem-oriented. Have faith
that, for every problem, there is
an inherent solution
awaiting discovery.

*B*e grateful for what you have,
however little it may seem to be.
Do not resent life for what it

hasn't given you, and you will
find abundance where you least
expected it.

*M*ake no apologies for yourself
when things go wrong. God
alone, after all, is infallible.

*Y*ou are the final measure of
anything you accomplish. That
work alone is noble which
ennobles its creator.

*M*eet every challenge from your
calm center within. Seek strength
and guidance intuitively, in your
inner Self.

Attune your limited human will to the infinite divine will.

Prize humility as you would the
Fountain of Youth. Pride is
the death of wisdom, and the
paralysis of every
worthwhile undertaking.

Winning People
to Your Ideas

*W*hen making a proposal, be deeply convinced, first, of its merits. Ask yourself, "Is this idea founded in truth?"

*I*t is not sufficient to believe in an idea. Be enthusiastic in your belief! But remember, enthusiasm is not excitement. It is deep conviction.

*N*ever tell an untruth. Let sincerity take such deep root within you that your simple word carries conviction.

*A*ddress the issues calmly, never emotionally or excitedly. To put

it otherwise: When you want
to be convincing, use
adjectives sparingly.

*C*reate a relaxed atmosphere.
Tension induces resistance to new
ideas. Relaxation, on the other
hand, fosters receptivity.

*L*ook for points of mutual
agreement before you proceed to
your central theme.

*U*nder attack, remain calm. Be
pleasant at all times. Withhold
recognition from comments that
are made simply to offend,

and be quietly firm in your
own convictions.

*Hold the thought that the other person,
too, is interested in arriving at the truth.*

Desire only that the truth prevail.
Be willing to change your mind
instantly, should the facts of a
matter prove you to be mistaken.

See yourself as the other person's
friend and well-wisher.

Put yourself in the other person's
shoes. Consider his or her point

of view (whether or not referring to it) before presenting your own.

Concentrate on the other person's needs in preference to your own.

Place less emphasis on the pronoun "I."

Appeal to people's altruism. Convince them of the universal benefits of your proposal.

Refrain from making leaps of logic for which your listener is not prepared.

*H*ave the patience to let others come to your position at their own time, and in their own way. (Reflect: It probably took *you* time, too, to arrive there.)

*B*e responsive to alternative suggestions.

*H*elp others to convince themselves. Don't overwhelm them with your enthusiasm.

*E*nter into your subject wholeheartedly. Make every word you speak important; give it your full concentration.

*D*evelop spontaneity. Don't hold doggedly to a point, if it no longer seems helpful or relevant.

*D*evelop creativity. Be willing at a moment's notice to explore new ideas.

*D*evelop magnetism. Project your convictions with the energy and conviction you yourself feel for them.

*N*ever retreat to a defensive position. If attacked for your ideas, counter good-humoredly, but with faith in them. Make no excuses for your sincere beliefs.

Never belittle the opinions,
however uninformed, of people
whom you are seeking
to convince.

Never plead, to your listener's
disadvantage, your own greater
knowledge or experience. Let
crystal clarity of vision be your
sole defense.

Support your statements with
convincing evidence. Avoid vague
claims, such as "Everybody
says so."

Keep discussion to the issues
as much as possible. Accept

diversions, when helpful for relaxing people's minds, but keep even those tethered firmly to the post of your true purpose.

*P*resent solutions. Don't diminish the energy of your presentation by dwelling unnecessarily on the problems connected with it. If problems exist, say so frankly, but give energy to resolving them.

*I*ntroduce your point early in your discussion. Don't keep your listeners in suspense, lest tension build within them and make them resistant to your ideas.

In any differences of opinion, look for points on which you can agree. Don't add to the confusion by replying with criticism or accusation.

If counterarguments exist, don't conceal them. Present them fairly; then place them in the context of a broader truth.

Forge lasting, not fragile, bonds with people, lest even in victory you lose their friendship and esteem.

Leadership

*L*eadership is an opportunity to serve. It is not a trumpet call to self-importance.

A leader should hold this thought constantly: "People are more important than things." Hold to that principle, and those who work with you will always give you their best.

*B*e loyal to those who work for you, whatever their position on the "totem pole." Loyalty inspires loyalty. By demanding loyalty of others first, you'll develop "yes-men," and the burden of every decision will rest on you alone.

*S*hare with others the credit for any work well done. You will then have their support in all you do. Support is given grudgingly to the leader who claims, "I did it all."

*T*ake from others the burden of blame. For even if the fault was theirs, in renouncing responsibility you renounce your leadership.

*M*ake truth the "bottom line" in your work, as in your life. Remember, only truth wins in the end.

*B*ear always in mind the larger picture. Ask yourself, "What are we *really* trying to accomplish?"

Many a short-term triumph has blocked the attainment of a long-term goal.

*L*earn even-mindedness. Be neither elated by success, nor depressed by failure. Let nothing that happens affect who you are, inside.

Concentrate on the work you are doing, not on yourself as its doer. Your ego can either infuse a project with energy, or hinder its execution, depending on whether you give the project energy, or hold it spinning in a vortex of self-adulation.

Never ask of others what you would not willingly do yourself. There are leaders, and there are bosses. Be one who leads, not one who drives others.

Leadership

Where your own well-being is concerned, be impersonal. Be personally concerned when it comes to the well-being of others.

Listen to the voice of reason, when others voice it. Tune in to the realities of every situation. Life teaches us through others, sometimes, or through circumstances. Be always ready to learn. You'll never lose face, if all you want is the truth.

Work with things as they are, not as you wish they were. The "impossible" dream can be attained only in *possible* stages.

Work with others' abilities as they are, not as you think they ought to be. Try to get the best person for the job at hand, but remember: "People are more important than things." Think also, "Is this job the best thing for the person under consideration for it?"

Develop farsightedness. Gaze past the visible toward potentials beyond the distant horizon.

Be solution-oriented, not problem-oriented. For each of these attitudes projects its own magnetism. Solution-orientedness attracts success. Problem-orientedness attracts only confusion and mental paralysis.

Leadership

Don't shackle yourself with habitual solutions. On the other hand, don't confuse merit with novelty. Do what is intrinsically right, even if has been done a thousand times, and it will seem always new.

Share with those under you your goals and ideals. Include them, as friends, in the dreams you

dream if you want their
constant support.

*A*ppeal to high principles. Don't
appeal to people's prejudices in
order to win their support.

*R*ecognize that high principles
include kindness and compassion.
Far down the line are such
considerations as rules and
precedents. People will often say,
"It's a matter of principle," when
what they intend is an appeal to
precedent. Precedent is often
made an excuse for not facing
with freshness and creativity the
realities and needs of the moment.

*T*he team you have working with you is more important than any product you are working on. Remember, a good team can develop many products.

Leadership

*D*o not allow your decisions to be influenced by your own likes and dislikes. The more you do so, the narrower your vision will become. Other people's likes and dislikes, however, are a necessary part of the reality you have to work with.

*I*nvite others' cooperation, rather than demanding their obedience. You can always, as the leader, enforce obedience. You will do so, however, at the cost of their willing and loyal support. Without these—indeed, without enthusiasm on their part—you will never receive their best efforts.

Be enthusiastic, first, yourself. Win others to your ideas by the joy you feel in them.

Be willing to do yourself whatever needs to be done.

Find joy more in the doing than in the things you do. You will then find that, although things change, your ability to inspire others will remain constant.

Carry everything you do toward some greater good. Allow no accomplishment to become an end in itself.

Leadership

Seek to inspire others with faith in their own high potential. Never speak belittlingly of them when they fall short of your expectations. Your faith in them, or your lack of it, will determine to a great extent the success of your endeavors.

Put your heart into everything you do. Don't give projects your merely reasoned endorsement.

Love others—not as separate entities from yourself, but as part of your own larger reality. Expand your reality to include others, and they will remain yours forever.

Why bear grudges? Be magnanimous. When people hurt you, remember that they hurt themselves even more. Give them your silent sympathy.

Maintain a sense of humor. At the same time, make it a point to laugh with others, never at them. If you must laugh at anyone, turn the laughter against yourself.

For Men

Give others the freedom to be themselves. Only thus will you feel really free to be *your*self.

Make demands of yourself, but be sensitive when making demands of others.

Place more reliance on the power of thought than on material prowess.

Think for yourself. Let no one do your thinking for you.

Don't drive others. Lead them sensitively to your point of view.

*B*e strong in yourself. In that way, you will give strength to others. Be like a spreading oak, to whose shade many come for shelter.

For Men

*B*e a sincere friend to all. Think in terms of how you can serve them, not of how they might be induced to serve you.

*S*trive for excellence in everything you do. Seek it not in competition with others, but as a thing worth achieving in itself.

*L*ive always by the truth. Give your word sparingly, but once you have given it, remain faithful to it

even in the teeth of a hurricane.
Where there is truth, there
is victory.

Don't take yourself too seriously.
There's a broad world out there,
far greater than you are. Go with
its flow, like a surfboard rider.
Know that the power lifting and
carrying you forward is much
greater than your own.

*Give less power to the thought of "I" and
"mine." You are an integral part of a much
greater reality.*

Temper the blade of reason in
the fire of practicality. Ask of any

idea, not that it be reasonable, merely, but that it work.

*B*e not relentless in your logic. For logic is only one way of arriving at the truth, whereas truth itself always transcends logic. Don't persuade by reason alone. For reason to be a friend, it must be guided by intuition.

For Men

*R*eason can be intuitive, when it consults the feeling in the heart to see whether a premise is right or wrong. Remove yourself somewhat from the opinions of others, and offer up your own opinions for the approval of your intuitive beliefs.

*L*ogic should not be used as a means for bullying people. Offer your reasons kindly, as a means of clarifying the issues under consideration.

*I*n any discussion, try always to be impartial. Make truth your guide, not the desire for victory. Indeed, see truth itself as the only victory worth winning.

*K*indness and consideration are proofs of inner strength. They are not symptoms of weakness. Consider with a fair mind points of view other than your own.

*I*n any undertaking, remember:
Self-conquest is the
greatest victory.

*B*e strong at your center; gentle
at your periphery.

*I*nner strength, in men especially,
depends far more than many
realize on sexual self-control.
Consider self-control, not self-
indulgence, the proof of
your masculinity.

*T*o transmute sexual energy, feel
it flowing up the spine from the
base to the brain. Much joy
accompanies this practice

*D*evelop willpower by accepting difficult challenges, then carrying them through to victory. Do something every day to exercise your willpower.

*B*e not afraid to follow your own star, though it shine for no one else.

*S*trengthen your magnetism by deepening your commitment, not by imposing your will on other people.

*B*e like a pine tree. Sink your roots firmly into the ground, but let your aspirations rise high into the sky of lofty ideals.

For Men

*L*et joy be the final goal of all your undertakings.

*B*e magnanimous in victory; in defeat, remain calm, self-contained, and ever hopeful of good. Allow neither victory nor defeat to define your reality. Defeat itself will then prove a kind of victory.

*R*espect others, if you want them to respect you.

*D*evelop graciousness and appreciation. These are marks of a refined nature. If you cede points to others you will win them as friends and lighten the burden of self-centeredness that is the chief obstacle to true success.

*D*evelop enthusiasm as a quality of your personality, not as a reaction to circumstances. Reason that lacks the support of feeling may be abstractly persuasive, but it is like an autumn leaf: beautiful perhaps, but bereft of life.

*B*e inspired by love, but ruled above all by truth, not by emotions.

*A*llow your heart's natural love to unfold, by renouncing selfishness, self-righteousness, and pride.

*E*xpand the love you feel for your own to include all others as your own.

For Women

*B*e true to yourself, and be less concerned with what others think of you. Don't accept their definitions of you, but grow into a self-definition of your own.

Give from your own strength. Depend less on the strengths of others. Develop your own talents, and don't envy other people theirs.

A vortex of disturbed emotions is often dissipated by a sense of humor, and a heartfelt laugh.

*T*ranscend your personal troubles by offering solace to other troubled hearts.

*R*emember: The greatest of all healers is love.

*D*eepen your receptivity, that you receive the experiences in your life on every level of your being. Let them gestate silently. Then offer them back, in the form of wisdom and new life for others.

*L*et your smiles be conceived in your heart, then given birth in the world through your eyes. Let your smiles be those of friendship, of healing, of appreciation.

*D*on't concentrate on drawing others by your beauty or by your feminine magnetism. For though it may be satisfying, at first, to find that you have this power over others, you will find, in time, that it diminishes you. Seek self-expansion, rather, by inspiring people—by appealing to the highest that is in them.

When you are tempted to utter caustic or sarcastic remarks, reflect: An excess of pepper can spoil a good meal. Hasty words have ruined many a precious friendship. But nothing is ever lost by kindness. Give others the freedom to grow at their own pace.

*E*xpand your capacity for loving into impersonal love for all humanity—for all life.

*N*urture others, and in the nurturing you will yourself be nourished from within. A wise man once said, "The channel is blessed by that which flows through it."

*S*ervice to others is not an indignity; it is a privilege. For by joyful service we renounce the pettiness of pride, and thereby attain inner freedom.

*W*henever we belittle others, we expose to them our own

insecurity. Graciousness to all is the clear echo of inner victories.

*T*o overcome a tendency to take things too personally, refer to impersonal principles what others say to you.

*W*hat we affirm in our hearts determines what we become. If we concentrate on littleness, we cannot avoid becoming petty. But if we concentrate on high thoughts and high ideals, we ourselves can achieve greatness.

*T*he way we look at life is colored by our feelings. A

negative mood can make even the color white look gray. A positive mood turns even a gray day into a thing of beauty. Live less in your moods. Let your feelings be impartial; keep them centered in the calmness within.

*W*omen are often highly intuitive, but their feelings must be kept calm, and grounded in receptivity. Intuition *is* calm, receptive feeling.

*P*ay more attention to the longer rhythms of life. Dwell less on the ups and downs of the moment; more on permanent realities.

Let your feelings be guided by wisdom, and your emotions by selfless love.

Give of yourself impersonally. Don't dwell on the thought of what others are giving—or are not giving—you.

True beauty is a radiance from within. It comes from kind, happy thoughts. It comes from virtuous qualities. Beauty is not a mask you wear to please others.

It is erroneous to make a cult of youth, for every age has its intrinsic beauty.

Show your appreciation. Show it more for whom the person is than for anything you are given.

*U*ntruth has no cohesion, no lasting power. Ignore people's criticisms, if they are wrong. If they are right, thank them (if only silently). Defeat unkindness by speaking well of those who sought to hurt you. The way to combat darkness is not to deepen the darkness, but to turn on the light.

*L*essen the number of your likes and dislikes. Find contentment in yourself, and in the lasting blessing of true friends.

*A*ct more. React less. Emotional reaction only clouds your understanding of reality. Let your love for others be like the compass needle, which, no matter how often it is deflected, returns always to the true North. Ground your behavior in what you consider right and true. Guide it by what you feel will give the greatest benefit to everyone.

*B*e concerned not with pleasing others, but with being a sincere friend to them.

*L*ife can be like a roller coaster ride—up one day, down the next—if you allow it to be. Act always from your inner center.

Whether things go well or ill,
reflect: All things change anyway.
Be neither elated nor depressed,
for nothing in this universe
remains the same forever. Change
becomes changelessness, the more
you live at your own center.

*P*ractice even-mindedness. Even-
mindedness flattens the bumps on
the road of life, and fills in the
potholes. Even-mindedness paves
the road, and ensures you a
smooth journey. The road that is
paved by even-mindedness is the
fastest highway to success.

*B*e fair. When conversing with
others, try to understand and
show respect for their points of

view. Only by understanding is there hope of changing anyone. Truth alone matters, ultimately, not your opinions.

*B*e to everyone, in a sense, a mother. Give to others unconditionally, and expect nothing from them in return. In this way, you will receive from Life a thousandfold.

When people hurt you, heal their sickness of disharmony by kindness, understanding, and forgiveness.

*T*raditionally feminine qualities are as strong in their own way as those which are more traditionally masculine. Air and water are as powerful as fire. Patient endurance, receptivity, and the ability to adapt to circumstances will often ensure victory where aggressiveness crashes in defeat.

For Women

Radiant Health
and Well-Being

*K*eep a proper, balanced diet. Eat foods rich in vitality. Study proper food combinations. Never overeat; rather, make it a practice to leave the table feeling that you could have eaten more.

*E*at in a harmonious environment, if possible, not in places where there is discord and confusion.

*K*eep a proper posture: Sit up straight; stand upright; hold your shoulders back, your chest up, your chin parallel to the ground.

*L*ive more in your spine. Your movements and gestures should flow outward from that inner center.

Radiant Health and Well-Being

*B*reathe properly. When walking, inhale and exhale deeply and rhythmically. As you breathe in, count to four; hold counting four, exhale to the same count; hold out four. Repeat this exercise (4-4-4-4) six to twelve times. Breathe consciously. Breathe deeply, from the diaphragm.

*E*xercise, to keep fit. Be conscious of the life-force that flows through your body as you move.

*L*ive in the awareness that you *are energy*. Bear in mind this principle: "The greater the will, the greater the flow of energy." Learn exercises that are designed to increase your flow of energy to the body; practice them regularly.

*P*ractice some meditation every day. From your own center of stillness, send stillness outward into your entire being.

*L*ove others—but impersonally, not with attachment. Attached love is self-love. It will tie you inwardly in knots. But impersonal love brings the body into perfect harmony. Pure love develops of itself, once the pettiness of

self-love has been eradicated
with kindness.

*B*e happy, within. Radiate
happiness outward with a sense
of total well-being to others.
Happiness is the fruit of faith
in life, in God, in your own
highest potentials.

*P*ractice willingness. Train
yourself to say "Yes," where
others say "No," or only
"Maybe."

*K*eep a positive, fearless attitude.
By affirming the highest good, you
will attract it to you always.

117

*E*njoy being in the fresh air. Breathe more consciously. With every breath, inhale vitality and courage into your mind and body; exhale stale thoughts, discouragement, and old habit patterns. Breathe in a sense of inner freedom; breathe out any lingering sense of bondage.

*B*e relaxed, both physically and mentally. Tension holds illness in the body, whereas relaxation releases and banishes it. To relax completely, first tense the body all over; then exhale forcibly and relax: *Feel* the tension leave your body. Mentally release all your cares and worries into the receptive vastness of space.

*K*eep good company. Mix with generous, energetic, joyful people—people who are interested in others and concerned for their well-being. Avoid the company of negative people, or of talking zombies. For the company you keep can magnetize you, and can also rob you of your magnetism.

*E*at more fresh, raw foods; fewer cooked foods; and no foods that are stale or overcooked. Remember, your food consists of much more than chemicals. Choose foods that are rich in life-force. Eat more fruits and vegetables, fewer meats.

*C*oncentrate on the vital essence in what you eat. For food is not only substance; it is also consciousness. Make it a practice to eat consciously, and the living vibrations in your food will fill your mind as well as your body, making you strong on all levels of your being. The more you eat consciously, the more, also, you will want to eat correctly.

*P*ractice self-control in all aspects of your life. Overindulgence only wastes vitality.

*B*ecome conscious of colors as channels of energy. Surround yourself with cheerful, harmonious colors. Inhale them mentally. Shun dark, "muddy," or depressing hues. When selecting foods, also, choose them for their diversity of colors. Color diversity in food will help ensure that your diet has the proper balance.

*B*e more conscious of sounds. When listening to music, concentrate on the consciousness that went into its composition. For music, whether calming or discordant, cheerful or depressing, affects the entire nervous system. It can make a person vital and responsive, or lifeless, dispirited, and resentful. Give preference to the music of composers whose awareness, as expressed through their music, is expansive.

*A*ffirm good health even in the face of illness. Positive affirmations, frequently repeated, will help to keep you radiant and strong. As your inner light shines brightly, illness will close its eyes and run away.

*I*magine yourself surrounded by an aura of light. Live more in the consciousness of this light. Expand it mentally. Include in it the people around you, the objects, the surrounding space.

*S*elf-involvement dulls the consciousness. Transcend it. Lessen your attachment to pettiness: to little rules of diet, to little fads. Expand your consciousness: Determine to live in inner freedom!

*B*e concerned for others' welfare. Expand your sympathies to include others in your radiant sense of happiness and well-being.

*P*ractice noninjury. Our well-being depends on the kind of thoughts we hold towards others. Injurious thoughts steel us to receive injury ourselves. Kind thoughts invite our nervous systems to relax; they promote self-healing and offer healing to all whom we meet.

Practice contentment, the supreme virtue. Contentment is the soil in which all other virtues flourish, the smooth leaf to which the raindrops of illness cannot cling.

*P*ractice cleanliness, inwardly as well as outwardly. Enjoy wholesome emotions, good thoughts, worthwhile activities. Disease thrives where there is impurity. But we flourish in health when we pay attention to cultivating purity—physically, mentally, emotionally, spiritually.

*P*ractice nonattachment. Nonattachment bestows inner peace, the precursor of

contentment; and relaxation,
the consort of good health.

*N*either envy anyone nor blame
anyone. Be at rest in your Self.
Bless all as you proceed serenely
on your way through life.

*B*e grateful—to life; to others.
Gratitude opens windows to
receive the sunlight of divine
abundance.

*L*et your energy flow upward,
toward the brain. Bend forward,
exhaling; then inhale slowly,
straightening up, and raise your
arms high above the head; feel life

vitalizing your body all the way to the fingertips. Gaze upward more often, and keep your awareness often focused at the front of your brain, midway between the eyebrows. Walk lightly. Sit lightly. Smile naturally.

*B*ecome a cause, not an effect. Let nothing condition your happiness. Accept from others only what you choose to accept: their good suggestions, but not their insistence on them; their constructive criticisms, but not their anger. Radiate outward into the world around you the light of your faith and wisdom.

Be a friend to all. When meeting people for the first time, think of them as your own.

Radiant Health and Well-Being

Emotional
Healing

*R*elinquish selfish desires by relating your emotions to a broader arc of feeling: love, for example, or concern for the needs of others.

*A*ffirm your inner freedom. Rejoice in it. Depend less on external circumstances.

*R*espect the right of others to come to their own decisions, and to make their own mistakes.

*O*vercome anxiety by doing your best in the present. Give up attachment to the outcome. Know that whatever is yours by right must come to you, sooner or later.

What is not yours by right will prove evanescent.

*O*vercome depression by useful activity, devoted selflessly to helping others.

Emotional Healing

*D*epression can be overcome, not by trying to reason your way out of a slump, but by vigorously raising your level of energy from the heart to the brain, then channeling it outward in creative activity and in useful service to others.

*B*anish depression by affirming mentally, "I am not my moods. Nor am I subject to the moods

131

of others. I am the ruler of my inner kingdom of thoughts and feelings!" Let everything you do originate in yourself, not in others. Don't allow yourself to be manipulated by circumstances.

*D*iscouragement can be overcome if you work to instill courage in others.

*R*ise above discouragement by not brooding. Act, instead! Uplift your heart's feelings. Stand upright; inhale, and with the inhalation draw courage upward from your heart to your forehead. As you exhale, cast out from your mind all mental weakness and negativity.

*C*rowd out loneliness by developing the company of inner "friends"—creative thoughts, high ideals, noble aspirations. Think of your mind as a nation, its thought-population composed of happy, self-motivated citizens.

Emotional Healing

*D*efeat loneliness by practicing the presence of God. Share with God (as Heavenly Father or Divine Mother) every thought, every feeling, every action.

*O*vercome unkind thoughts by reflecting that the person you hurt most whenever you are not charitable is yourself. The principal recipient of your

kindness, on the other hand,
will also be yourself.

*H*urt feelings can be reduced to
insignificance by reducing your
personal expectations of others,
and of life. When you demand
nothing of others, their words and
actions will find you always
inwardly at peace.

*Overcome hurt feelings by directing your
attention outward, in giving of yourself to
others, instead of dwelling self-centeredly
on what you want from them.*

*L*ighten cynicism by
concentrating on the needs of

others. Dwell no longer on the thought that life, or other people, owe it to you to be other than what they are.

*T*ransform bitterness into contentment by not feeling that you deserve more from life than it is giving you. You will always find meted out to you exactly as much as you have earned from life.

*O*vercome dependence on others by this reflection: Can I gain anything from others that doesn't resonate with something I already possess in myself? Live more from within, and from that center radiate your own special strength and courage to the world.

Confront discontentment with the thought that conditions are, essentially, always neutral. The pleasure or displeasure they give us depends on our own mental attitudes. Determine, therefore, to be ever happy in yourself.

Confound doubt by concentrating on all the reasons you have in life for being grateful. Don't focus on the things that seem to you imperfect. Habitual doubt is a manifestation of self-centeredness. Love truth. *Love!* Fill your heart with generous sentiments, and doubt will flee like night shadows before the sunrise.

*L*ighten the tendency toward mental dullness by training yourself to say "*Yes!*" instantly, whenever your first impulse is to grumble or to say "No." Welcome life in all its fascinating variety and challenges. Keep your heart open, like a flower in full bloom, to life's experiences. Overcome the tendency within you toward feelings of rejection and reactive withdrawal.

Emotional Healing

*D*rive out fear by living at that calm center within you where nothing on earth can touch you: not fire, nor flood, nor loss of any kind—not even death.

*L*ift yourself above guilt feelings by relinquishing the past. What has been done is done; it belongs to the past. Resolve to do better from today onward—better and ever better, until that better becomes the very best that is in you. View your mistakes as prods, simply, to ultimate victory.

*S*atisfy greed by maintaining inner contentment, and by harmonizing the feelings of the heart. Affirm mentally: "I am complete in myself. I am free from all anxiety and need! Contentedly I accept whatever comes to me, while doing my best to achieve my valid goals."

*S*oothe the tendency toward irritation by viewing life in its

138

longer rhythms: not the little ripples of pleasure and pain, but the broad waves of long-term commitments; and not emotional commitments merely, but the great ocean swells of dedication to high ideals.

Emotional Healing

*D*rive out negativity by recognizing that what you behold in the world reflects back to you what you are, yourself. Work at self-transformation. Never think that the world owes it to you to grant your every wish, but concentrate, rather, on what you have to give to the world.

*E*xpand your little base of insecurity by visualizing yourself

seated at the heart of infinity.
Reflect: The whole universe, as
far as your own awareness is
concerned, has its center in
yourself. Send forth healing rays
of faith and good will to all. Life
will sustain you in every difficulty,
if you live more consciously at the
center from which your own
life flows.

Defuse jealousy by realizing that
no human being ever owns
another. Everyone stands alone
before eternity. That one most
truly loves who is free inside, and
who grants the same freedom to
all. Grow at your own pace. Give
others the same freedom. Each of
us must, in his own time, find his
rightful position in the great
scheme of things.

*L*augh at self-conceit by viewing the universe as having its center everywhere, its circumference nowhere. Each human being lives at the heart of a vast reality. Each has a need for a personal approach to truth. The needs of others in this respect are just as important as your own.

Emotional Healing

*D*estroy resentment with the affirmation, "I am free inside!" Wish freedom for all. Radiate kindness outward from your heart's center to all. Become a source of happiness to others, and you will know joy.

*D*rown self-pity in the recognition that emotional self-indulgence only limits your ability to accomplish anything.

Remember, whatever any human being has ever achieved, *you* can achieve. What is necessary is only patience, sensitive insight, and determination. Every seeming limitation is but an opportunity to achieve shining victory.

Banish low self-esteem by realizing that you are an integral part of all that is. You are sustained forever by the Power that brought the universe into existence. Open your heart to life. Cease seeing yourself as a lonely plant, drooping and waterless on an arid desert.

Relinquish the fear of failure by not being attached to success.

Concentrate, rather, on the willpower and energy necessary for success. Even your failures can become stepping-stones to greater achievements.

Conquer the fear of death by deepening your awareness of that central part of your being which never changes, but weaves like a thread through life's tapestry of change. The consciousness of change is allied to the fear of death. But to see changelessness at the heart of change is the secret of immortality.

Emotional Healing

Self-Acceptance

*T*he secret of self-acceptance is not contraction inward upon the ego: It is self-expansion.

*O*pen your heart to life; *embrace* it! At the same time, never hold the thought, "*I* am embracing life." Tell yourself, instead, "It is *life* I am embracing!"

*E*xpand your sense of self to include others. Rejoice with them in their joys. Grieve for them in their sorrows, while trying gently to lead them from sorrow toward wisdom and true happiness.

*G*aze in appreciation upon the world around you. Never enter

self-assertively into conflict with
it. Self-acceptance comes from
cheerfully embracing your own
role in the greater scheme
of things.

Self-Acceptance

Self-acceptance comes through
acknowledging that you are an
integral part of the universe. You
can never separate yourself from
that totality; nor can it ever
separate itself from you. As you
need it, to function properly,
so does the universe need you.
Everlastingly, if need be, it awaits
your harmony and your love.

Self-acceptance comes from trying
to understand, rather than to be
understood; trying to relate to,

rather than to be related to. It comes from giving of yourself empathetically to all.

*S*elf-preoccupation creates a psychological vortex; it distorts your preceptions, and robs you of your capacity for happiness. Give up self-preoccupation by relaxing its centripetal pull; offer its energies outward into the great ocean of life around you. Offer up your personality conflicts for resolution, like dissonant chords, into the great harmony that is All Life.

*C*oncentrate not on how others treat you, but on how you treat them; on what you can do to help them.

Which have you found to be more self-fulfilling: self-contraction, or self-expansion? Study the consequences of each. Contractiveness imposes limitations on the mind, which bring suffering. Expansiveness, however, dissolves limitations; it transforms every sorrow into joy.

Self-Acceptance

Self-acceptance comes from meeting life's challenges vigorously. Don't numb yourself to your trials and difficulties, nor build mental walls to exclude pain from your life. You will find peace not by trying to escape your problems, but by confronting them courageously. You will find peace not in denial, but in victory.

*W*hen you shrink mentally inward upon yourself, your problems loom larger and more menacing, for you become diminished in your own eyes. But when you expand your consciousness to accept broader visions of reality, you gain strength and stature in your own eyes. As your problems become dwarfed, you find you can face and conquer them.

*I*s it really so difficult to accept yourself? Whom is it, really, that you can't accept? Not your inner self, certainly. Rather, your rejection is of your own sense of littleness, your diminished self-identity. Lose yourself in an enlarging vision of the great adventure that is life!

Self-Acceptance

*B*e childlike. Don't judge: *Accept.* By blaming others you enter a mode of self-contraction, and only inflict pain on yourself. Accept others as they are. Accept life as it is. By learning acceptance, you will learn above all to accept yourself. With acceptance will come forgiveness, and a joyful sense of inner release.

*D*o you want to learn self-acceptance? Then don't begin with affirmations of self-worth. Such affirmations only encourage personal comparisons with other people: "I'm just as worthy as he is"; "I'm *more* worthy than he is!"; "He's preventing me from developing a sense of my own worthiness!" You will find in self-forgetfulness a more effective cure for self-rejection.

The way to self-acceptance is to affirm generous, self-giving attitudes toward others. Only by including them in your own reality can you develop the capacity to see yourself accurately in respect to all life.

Once you have developed an expansive attitude, affirm your nondependence on others. Affirm inner freedom in a spirit of joyful equality with all.

*B*ear in mind that you, like every other human being, are unique. Your role on Life's great stage will be played by no one else. Discover who you *really* are, behind the ever-changing masks your little ego wears.

*R*ealize your uniqueness in the entire universe. No one will ever have your song to sing: Through all eternity it is yours alone. Your primary task in life is to learn that song, and to sing it perfectly.

*A*ccept others, first, as *they* are. Only then will you be able to accept yourself as *you* are.

*D*on't envy others their talents and accomplishments. It is better even to fail in your own soul-appointed duty than to succeed in someone else's. Once you succeed in being wholly yourself, you will have achieved the most glorious success possible for any human being.

*R*esent no one. By resenting others we only belittle ourselves.

*D*evelop respect for everyone. For as we are, so do we imagine others to be; and whatever we imagine in others, we reinforce in ourselves.

Mix with those who, in their expansiveness, offer support to others. Shun the company of those whose contractiveness makes them cynical or insecure.

Love others. Do not wait for them first to love you.

Serve others in the awareness that you can serve as an instrument of a Higher Power.

Forgive others. For as we forgive, so are we ourselves forgiven by them—and by Life itself. In

forgiveness we acquire the
wisdom to forgive *ourselves*.

Don't expect too much of others.
Thus, you will learn not to expect
too much of yourself.

We should not blame others for
their negative attitudes and
behavior toward us. For in
blaming them we only weaken
ourselves, and give others power
over us.

Rise above self-blame.
Remember, the more important
the painting, the longer the time

and the greater the effort required
to carry it to perfection.

*U*proot negative expectations
from the mind. Sow positive ones,
for like attracts like. Your destiny
is to a great extent molded by the
expectations you hold of life.

Self-Acceptance

*D*o not give yourself too much
importance, nor take yourself too
seriously. Your true importance
will increase proportionately
to how little of it you claim
for yourself.

*E*xpand your sense of selfhood.
Include others in your larger Self.

View their happiness, their fulfillment, their successes as your own.

Don't take your mistakes too seriously. Calmly determine that you will simply do better next time.

Do not identify yourself with your mistakes. They are not yours, but were simply there to be made by anyone striving sincerely toward perfection.

Don't identify yourself with failure. Neither success nor failure can define you, who are made in the image of Infinite Perfection.

Self-Acceptance

*R*aise your level of energy by developing an attitude of willingness. Do willingly and cheerfully whatever needs doing.

*G*et sufficient exercise. Breathe deeply; sit and stand erect. Eat a preponderance of fruits and vegetables; less meat. A healthy body makes for healthy attitudes in life.

*K*eep a sense of humor. Above all, learn to laugh at yourself; it will give you a right sense of proportion. Read one funny story a day. Share at least one good joke every day with your friends.

*T*ake full responsibility for whatever happens to you. Nothing occurs without a cause, one that usually can be traced to some attitude, some expectation —perhaps held only subconsciously—in our own minds.

*D*on't allow the weeds of guilt to grow in the garden you are cultivating of faith in yourself. Reflect: Human beings are prone to error. Transform feelings of

guilt into a resolution to do
constantly better.

*L*augh with others, if they tease
you. Don't take their words too
deeply to heart.

*K*eep a positive attitude. A wise
man once said, "Conditions are
essentially neutral. Your attitude
determines whether they are
positive or negative for you."

*D*on't try too hard to justify
yourself in others' eyes. Be
complete in yourself. Do your
best by your own understanding;

then accept the consequences with equanimity. Bear in mind that the highest Judge of your behavior resides forever in yourself.

Never condition your happiness, nor the truths that you hold dear, by the opinions of others.

Remain centered in your inner reality. Do not allow yourself to be victimized by other people's definitions of what is right or wrong.

Be concerned with pleasing God and your own higher conscience—not other people, except as they may help to clarify or confirm for you the Higher Will.

Self-Acceptance

*B*e grateful for whatever tests you attract in life, for they are means by which you can grow in strength and wisdom.

*C*oncentrate on your potential for self-improvement. Love that potential, rather than your present state of imperfection. Affirm that what is yours *potentially* is yours already, and forever.

Comfort and Joy

Love all; for by loving we live in joy, but in hating and in resenting others we experience only pain.

Understand wherein true satisfaction lies: not in change, but in stillness; not in things, but in one's deeper Self. With the psalmist, sing: "He leadeth me beside the still waters."

Show mercy, when you know that you have the power to avenge a wrong. "Blessed are the merciful, for they shall receive mercy."

Open your heart in silence to the power of love. A saint once said,

166

"If you knew how much God loves you, you would die for joy!"

Greet every trial with a resolute smile of approaching victory. "There are no such things as obstacles: There are only opportunities!"

Comfort and Joy

Give joy to others—with a kind smile; with a word of encouragement, of appreciation.

Do some one thing *today* to bring solace to some grieving soul. Serve all as a channel for God's solace.

Concentrate on the qualities you like and admire in your friends.

Recall the times when others have given to you sincerely of themselves.

Think of ways that you might bring comfort to others; then implement those thoughts through action, by giving comfort to all.

Pray for someone who sees himself as your enemy. Offer your own feelings toward him up to God.

*B*e centered in changelessness. Let nothing disturb you, nothing frighten you. All things pass. Live in the thought of eternity.

*K*eep your mind fixed on life's highest priority. Make God your polestar, and the ship of your life will never stray far from its course.

*A*ffirm joy in yourself. Don't wait passively for joy to come to you.

*R*emember, joy belongs to the present. It belongs to *today*. Don't

wait for joy to be yours at some
hoped-for time in the future.

Understand the difference
between fulfilled desire and
true joy.

Seek joy not in the fluctuations
of emotion, but in the calmness
beneath them. As it says in
Scripture, "Comfort ye
your hearts."

Understand that both comfort
and joy are the companions of a
peaceful conscience.

*U*nderstand that the highest joy
comes from God. It cannot
be merely affirmed: It must
be received.

*S*ee joy as the fruit not of
excitement, but of inner peace.

*E*xpand whatever bubble of joy
you feel, until it fills your being.
Then expand it beyond your
confines to touch the lives
of others.

*T*hank God daily—not so much
for His gifts as for His love.

See God's love behind the trials of life. Fear them not: Only by combat does the warrior become strong.

Accept no failure as destiny's final decree. A wise man said: "The season of failure is the best time for planting the seeds of success."

Live courageously from today onward. Forget the past. A backward glance shows everyone something he did that shames him. But your future will improve if you do your best, with courage, from now on.

*L*ook upon your family as God's gift to you.

*F*orgive those who have deeply hurt you. In forgiveness lies joy. When we refuse to forgive others, however, we discover that it is no longer possible to forgive ourselves.

Comfort and Joy

❦

*S*ee God's love behind the gift of human love.

*R*eflect: You belong to no one, and no one belongs to you. True, selfless love is the gift of inner freedom.

*R*ejoice in the happiness
of others.

*C*omfort and joy are states of
consciousness. They are
not produced by
physical circumstances.

Bringing Peace to Earth

*R*emember, whatever peace you bring to the earth must begin at that little piece of earth on which *you* stand.

*F*irst, calm the feelings in your own heart.

*E*manate consciously, from your heart, rays of peace into the world around you.

*S*urround yourself, wherever you go, with an aura of peacefulness. Walk consciously in that light.

*T*ouch others daily with the wand of your inner peace.

*L*ive less at your periphery, more at your heart center.

*T*ouch others at their center, by reaching out to them across a bridge of light from your own heart.

*T*hink *peace* when you look into people's eyes.

*S*end peace into the world by consciously projecting a calming influence through your voice.

*L*et your every movement be an expression of your inner peace and harmony.

*R*ealize that peace, when you express it, has its source not in you, but in Infinity.

*U*nderstand that true peace is never passive; that, like nourishing rain, it sustains whatever life it touches.

*S*eek, wherever possible, points of discussion on which you and others can agree.

*N*ever try to make peace at the cost of true and high principles.

*N*ever place expediency above truth.

Understand that love is the highest truth, the highest principle.

Light a candle of kindness in your heart, whenever you feel a need to correct someone. Then, as you speak, hold it there unwaveringly.

Forgive any who have ever wronged you. Indeed, if you cannot offer peace to them, how will you offer it to others, whose lives have never touched yours?

Don't demand that others live as you believe they should. But live unassumingly by your own beliefs.

*B*ear in mind that the world simply *is* what it is. And is it so small a place, that you intend to change it radically? Live at peace with yourself, if you would bring peace to even one other human being.

*R*ecall that the promise of peace came down to earth from heavenly regions. It has never been the gift of governments.

*R*eflect that peace comes not from outer, but from inner, victories.

*R*eflect that one single peace-inspired, peace-inspiring thought

holds more power for peace than
a thousand shouted slogans.

*P*lace a higher priority on holding
peace in your heart than on doing
all those little things that daily cry
out for your attention.

*A*ccept that creating peace is
not a job for others, only: It is
your responsibility.

*D*o not wait for the future to
bring you peace. Live peacefully
this moment. Then extend that
peacefulness from day to day as
you live into the future.

*L*ive this day *well* and nobly,
with kind thoughts toward all.

*R*elinquish selfish desires, and
thereby establish peace and
freedom in your own heart.

*P*lace more faith in Divine Law
than in human laws.

*L*ive by the spirit, not by the
mere letter, of God's law.

*P*ray daily for world peace—not as an end to strife and discord, merely, but as the dawn of Divine Love on earth.

**Bringing
Peace
to
Earth**

Meditation

*M*editation is the necessary complement of prayer. Prayer is talking to God. Meditation is listening for His answer. Without both of these ingredients, divine conversation is impossible.

*M*editation is including God in *your* reality.

*M*editation is possible only in perfect stillness. How can God hold a meaningful discussion with you if you keep on interrupting?

*S*tillness, in meditation, is not a mental vacuum. It is rapt attention.

Attention, in meditation, must be of the heart as well as of the head. If it is mental only, it becomes either voracious or too abstract. If it is of the feelings only, it becomes emotional and therefore restless. The heart's feeling should be directed upward toward the seat of intellect at the point between the eyebrows.

Meditation

Meditation should be expansive, not contractive. Begin your meditation with a prayer that the whole planet be blessed.

Contractiveness is a manifestation of ego-consciousness. The ego is centered in the medulla oblongata at the base of the brain. Focus your attention there, until you cognize that as your human center of awareness. Then relax that focus; release your attention to flow forward in concentration toward the point between the eyebrows.

When the upward-flowing energy gets blocked in the medulla oblongata, it reinforces the ego. Relax the energy in the medulla, that the energy flow onward and outward ever more expansively.

Do not think, in meditation, "How can the Divine serve my desires?" Think, rather, "How can I give myself more perfectly to Thee?"

God is both personal and impersonal. In relation to you, He is very personal, but His infinite reality is impersonal. In your relation to Him, therefore, strive to become more and more expansively impersonal. Love Him for Himself, not for yourself. He who made you made also the stars and galaxies, spinning on mighty tides of infinite space.

Meditation

Relinquish outward attachments. Affirm divine freedom within.

Sit upright with a straight spine; feel that your strength emanates from your spine rather than from the muscles of your body.

Hold your body perfectly still. Gradually free yourself from the compulsion to move.

Deeply relax your body: Inhale, tense the body; throw the breath out and relax. Release into the surrounding atmosphere, like wisps of vapor, any lingering eddies of tension that you feel.

Feel space in the body, and gradually expand that feeling from the body outward, into infinite space.

Focus your gaze and attention at the point between the eyebrows— the seat of ecstasy in the body.

Pray with deep faith—not as an outsider to heaven, but as one whose true, eternal home is there.

Meditation

Sing to God, out loud or silently, to awaken devotion in the heart.

Love God in whatever form you hold especially dear. Pray, "God—my Father, Mother, dearest Friend—I am Thine forever: Thine alone!"

Offer gifts of love upward from your heart to the point between the eyebrows, like the soaring flames in an all-purifying fire.

191

*D*well on the thought of great saints, past and present, who have known God; attune your consciousness to theirs.

*R*adiate blessings from your heart outward to all the world.

*P*ut resolutely aside every plan, every project, and focus on the moment. The world will be there still, when you finish your meditation!

*E*nter instantly into the silence within. Do not waste precious time in mental wandering.

Send any vagrant thoughts in your mind soaring, like little balloons, upward through skies of Infinity until they disappear in the blue distance.

Meditation

≪

Release yourself from the limitations of body and ego; identify yourself with Infinity.

Visualize God in an eternal aspect—as infinite light; cosmic sound; eternal peace, love, or joy; seek to unite yourself with God in that aspect.

Affirm contentment. Don't expect God to do all the work of

bringing you out of darkness into
infinite light and joy.

*D*well on the thought of God's
love for you. Destroy in a bonfire
of devotion any lingering doubts
you have.

*P*ractice single-minded
concentration. Be absorbed in the
peace within.

*M*ake yourself ever more
receptive to divine grace, in full
awareness that God's power alone
will liberate your soul.

*O*ffer yourself up wholly to God, holding nothing back.

*V*isualize your breath as a flow of energy in the spine, upward with inhalation, and downward with exhalation, until the flow seems a mighty river.

*V*isualize the energy in the spine rising in joyful aspiration toward the point between the eyebrows.

*L*isten intently to any sounds you hear in the inner ear; become absorbed in them.

*V*isualize yourself seated at the heart of eternity; send rays of divine love outward from your center to all the universe.

*B*e steadfast in your practice, for the more you meditate, the more you will want to meditate, but the less you meditate, the less will you find meditation attractive.

Affirm that you already are *those high truths toward which you aspire: inner peace, divine love, and perfect joy.*

*U*nify your inner and your outer life: Offer every problem up for resolution to the peace within;

allow that peace to infuse your outward activities.

*K*eep your concentration positive; never meditate to the point of fatigue or boredom.

Meditation

*S*ee God as the sole Doer. Seek His guidance in everything you do.

About the Author

When not traveling and lecturing throughout the world, Mr. Walters resides near the town of Nevada City, California. There in a beautiful forest setting surrounded by the majestic beauty of the Sierra Nevada foothills, he expresses his lifelong dedication to clarity.

With a reputation worldwide as a teacher, writer, composer, singer, photographer and administrator, his principal interest is to show how the secrets of life are available to all who choose to listen inwardly for them.